Islands Are But Mountains

*title.*

# ISLANDS
# ARE
# BUT
# MOUNTAINS

*subtitle.*

## New poetry from the United Kingdom

PLATYPUS PRESS, England

*Islands Are But Mountains* © Platypus Press, 2019
All poems copyrighted to the individual poets.
All works used by permission. All rights reserved.

ISBN 978-1-913007-03-4

First Edition, 2019

10 9 8 7 6 5 4 3 2 1

Cover and interior design by Peter Barnfather
Cover photography by Mirko Nicholson
    & Mitchell Orr
Type set in Bergamo Pro, FontSite Inc.

A CIP catalogue record for this book
is available from the British Library

Published by Platypus Press

Printed & bound by Clays Ltd, Elcograf S.p.A.

# ONE

# TWO

## THREE

# FOUR

# ONE

*"the fault turned out to be mine"*

*Mary Jean Chan*

# Song

When hypervigilance is a hymn you cannot
refuse, remember that the pilgrimage from
hurt to healing winds, like a lover's footsteps
through sand as she meanders: the sudden
slip, the inevitable fall. Wonder what songs
are left after the mothers have gone to bed
and the world is lighter without their grief.
Recall the questions all mothers ask their
own children: *Are you happy, will you come
home?* Far away from her, you will discover
another kind of love: its wide pavements and
cul-de-sacs, a boundless sky, torrential rain
smoothing the pebbles, loss weathering away.

*Remi Graves*

# Strong

To grip your hips as you bend, opening the oven,
to press myself not quite into you, but close—
is to know exactly who I want
and still be shadow-boxing the shape of such muscular lust.

I grapple with the thought of holding you tighter.
In the midday light, when it is impossible not to glimpse
the tree trunk shadow my body casts over yours,
when I am just a branch, made strong by what is heavy:
the guilt of wanting you the way they say men do.

I'd like to shut my eyes like you do,
let them roll back into silence and feeling,
swap the fears I have yet to name for
the taste of skin, lips, shared breath.

You pull the oven door shut,
and I am still in awe
of the way you trap heat.

*Natalie Linh Bolderston*

# Triệu Thị Trinh,
## *or The Lady General Clad in Golden Robe*

I learn flight from every wingless thing,
pull the sky down to meet me.

Summer clenches around my womb.
I barter for my child–skin and lose.

I want to believe I was named for my mother,
that I gasped whole from her body, full–tongued

and armoured. I want to believe that I wear her face
to every war, fight with the anger of our failed gods.

I scream from an elephant's head, and women remember
the taste of their teeth. I lead us through mountains,

navigate by moon–spattered blade, measure distance
in bodies and crows. With their eyes closed,

any of these men could be my father. Each one
a felled ox, rain searching for an opening in their chests.

They feed me their ghosts hair by hair, tooth by tooth.
I reach into my body and pull at their bloodless voices

as if they want to be found, as if they saw me and knew
the only way home was to fall.

Oh mother, I have learned so much without you,
so why is every sound a broken wing? Why

do I remember every place I've knelt in prayer,
rinsed blood from my mouth? I want to tell

how it will end: my golden armour
the only body I have left, begging you,

*please, don't die without me.*

*Dean Atta*

# My School Blazer Hangs
# on the Corner of a Gravestone

*Do you do poppers?* he asks.
I think of tiny plastic cannons
about to be pulled, of balloons
about to drop from the ceiling,
of a Teenage Mutant Ninja Turtles
birthday cake when I was six.

I'm sixteen now, high on weed,
about to have sex in a graveyard.
He hands me a small glass bottle
full of liquid, I unscrew the top
but don't know what to do next.
*Do I drink it?* I ask, innocently.

*No, you hold it under your nose*
*and inhale; it helps you relax.*
I follow his instructions. A chemical
explosion in my brain, streamers
burst forth into a tangled rainbow,
then all fades to black. I collapse.

When I awake, his eyes reflect me:
a zombie rising from a grave.
I feel like an empty plastic cannon,
party debris, balloon shrapnel.
Later, at my grandparents' house,
dinner is waiting for me. Nobody asks

about the mud on my trousers.
My red eyes. My missing school blazer.

*Alycia Pirmohamed*

# Self-Portrait with Fish Eyes

I am a woman who is *longdark*
language

a woman who eats fish eyes
to feel close to mother

a woman who loves whole milk
whole figs and single dimensions—

I am a woman with *this* many faces
*this* being not a number

but a rhizome of turmeric
eyelashes sweeping

against the smoke
a lily's open mouth

my voice
                such tall spruce

I am a woman that carried
my first heartache

before I was born—
a woman whose irises are

split open seams
spilling a *longdark* bloodline

a woman disguised
as a healed wound

a daughter splintered by every
memory crossed

*Jemilea Wisdom-Baako*

## Grey Coats & Nokia Phones

today you beg to be finished with this era of childhood
finished with the shades of dull & the boys on pushbikes

outside your window this morning    you find an old cigarette
in the inside pocket of your coat    put it to your lips    pretend

your mother called you a different name    whispered it into soil
grew a girl as rebellious as Japanese knotweed    spread wildly

determined not to be cut    roots too thick to be plucked into pretty
or passiveness or purity    but your stems are scattered into wind

because you are wasteful & you cannot grow breasts
even your womanhood is ignoring your calls    so you gasp into

daylight hoping your mouth will burst open a song to rid you
of the awkwardness of waiting    watching    wanting to age

faster    to feel seen by the boys on pushbikes who gather
like prayer meetings on Tuesday nights    even in the rain

who utter prophecies in new era hats on grime beats
even they have learnt the necessity of a name change

you swallow hard like Gemma behind bike sheds
take the shortcut down the alley in the dark

because you are bad at making decisions you find men
who do not care that your age hasn't bloomed

    who are puzzled at the fear in your brow as they chase
what you hold between your thighs    as if you are woman

    don't make eye contact with the devil    though he stares
promising to grant wishes    run    don't tell him your name

*Sara Hirsch*

# How to Move Country

Buy five vintage suitcases from a friend on Facebook
who used them decoratively for her travel themed wedding,

joke to yourself that her maiden name was Case—
try the joke out on the Uber driver,

exist in that silence until you get your cases home.
Ensure three of the handles immediately break,

empathise with them. Only bring what you can fit
in three cases unfit for travel. Ignore the weight limit—

overfill until the leather stretches out of shape,
give away most of your things, tell your mother,

exist in that silence. Pack your guilt in the smallest box,
pack the key and hope it gets lost. Do not cry. Not yet.

Reread the shipping instructions. Remove most of your items
and repack them to redistribute the weight:

mainly the books, bring all of your books and none of your bedding,
everywhere sells bedding, but these poets have what you need

to sleep soundly when everything is upside down.
Start buying stuff you don't need. Bulky jumpers,

books you have already owned and given away,
overfill your pockets with stuff, anchors to keep you rooted

to everything you have ever known. Consider staying.
Feel the pull of this place, then redistribute the weight.

Visit the grave once before you go. Exist in that silence
until it stretches out of shape. Leave a stone at the base,

take another home in your pocket, then redistribute the weight.
Say goodbye to your mother, feel heavy with her helplessness,

wait for her to cry, wait,           redistribute the wait,
    wait,                              wait.

*Omotara James*

# Exhibition of the Queered Woman

you said
you'd turned me

just as
you'd turned

others,
women who'd loved

you before,
you meant changed

which is
an active verb:

to change form
or state or color

△

in nature
(specifically fall)

when we say
leaves turn

what we mean
is die

which is
synonymous

with become;
i came

to love your
begging

me to stay
through

your states
of illness, your

open and broken
marriages

△

we exchanged
promises

without an
audience

before begging
off

i was wrong
to think

i understood
how

the wheels
in your head

turned,
the act

of moving
in circular directions

around an axis,
was always

the point

△

in water

the switch from low
to high tide

signals
sea birds

to forage
at night

△

the fault
turned out

to be
mine, my turn

now, as in
an opportunity

to break
for sanity

to swallow
a bruise

that begins
in dark blue

lurching towards
context

*Rowan Evans*

## tide ritual

now the kneeling
    at water's edge

    *at break of day | whiteness*

  *the year is ending*

    the spine, the bone
  forming routes of
impulse to direction,
    image of becoming

      self's flood-remnant

    the shore, the instruction
  vanishing

    now the kneeling body's
prone curve,
    the wearer, the shedding

      *in the final stage*
*the face contacts the water*

*Jennifer Lee Tsai*

# The Meaning of Names

Your surname comes from the Old English word,
*lēah*, for meadow or forest clearing—

your love is an airy space which holds me
in both light and shade.

At our wedding banquet, my mother wrote
our surnames in gold on firecracker-red paper

with the symbol for double happiness, 囍,
rejoiced at how your English name,

the character for a plum tree, 李,
sounded the same as her mother's.

Legend says that a minister's son
of your name escaped with his mother

from the cruelty of an emperor
and survived only by eating plums.

I'm loath to relinquish my surname, 徐,
which tells me how I want us

to live our lives together, slowly, gently,
my name which came from my father

and grandfather—an immigrant who carried it
on his lengthy crossing, anglicised it

unrecognisably to what it sounds like in essence,
a breath. Their marble headstones

have two sets of names, as will mine.

*Alycia Pirmohamed*

# Fire Starter

This is the hum
of a northern forest.

Don't forget all of the salt
that has gone into this healing—

wince if you must,

call out to India for two hundred years
if you must.

I am building a home and
burning down

my body that has never felt
like my body,

drinking from a spring
to balance

all of this smoke.

I am building a fire
that snags

onto the redwoods.

I want to redesign this dish
my body was

born into,
cardamom and brown skin

multiplying within the agar.
Hair that smells

like burning grass,
a landscape that reaches for

another land.

# TWO

*"Years before, the whole garden ignites"*

*Emily Blewitt*

# 13 weeks, 2 days

I don't know how to say it,
but there you were—little ghost
in my ceiling, floating
on your side. The outline
of your slim hips, strung spine
stretched lazily in the same position
I sleep some nights, facing away
from your father. We watched you refuse
to show us your nose. You offered
your crown instead, crossed and uncrossed
your arms and legs, dipped
upside-down. You were turning
the way a seal rolls underwater
for joy. You were radiant
and reluctant to share. The midwife said
this was your place, that we were

just visiting. When finally
you lay on your back, a small otter
cradling clam and rock, she was quick
as a heron slipping a fish to the gullet
to capture your image. She had to be.
You were elusive. A natural phenomenon
observed perhaps twice. Luminous
like algae on the water,
like Northern Lights.

*André Naffis-Sahely*

# The Carpet That Wouldn't Fly

*for my brother*

You sport the sickly ecstasy of the exiles
that people your mother's favourite novels:
quiet, pale-faced, consumptive dreamers.
Your feet, once accustomed to soft sand,
fall heavier now. You lament the peculiar

European fetish for marble, its coldness.
Sometimes at night, in between cigarettes,
you paced the balcony, clapped your hands,
as if expecting the cheap rug beneath you,
to flout reason and fly you back to the past.

*Bryony Littlefair*

# Lido

Seeing you at the lido was
like walking past a house I used to live in.

Wondering at the blind windows, the grass
just trimmed, the doorstep a brave new red.

Inside things murmur. A drawer sighs shut.
Somebody fishes onion from the plughole,

wet and nauseous between their fingers.
Somebody showers, tilting their face

for a moment to the faucet. Somebody
unsheathes a new record from its case

and music fills the room and it's terrible
and someone is dancing

like they've got no bones, like they don't have
anywhere to be. You looked up just once

then down quickly, then walked on.

Leo Boix

# A Fable

Backward from palms, she creates unknown life—
half human, half crustacean—into the world
she knows well: pools filled with golden toads,
porcelain sea-monsters, snails listening to sins,
a procession of mosquito larvae, squirming.
Morphed woman, with one-spanned slate wing,
circling Aconcagua's conquering peak, to see
this world upside down. Once she is christened,
her ears will be pierced, her hair coloured dark:
the sea-hawk goddess. Before giving birth at dusk,
orange nocturnal bonfire, to her black-necked spawn,
the criollo chant: *Para que no se te muera nunca!*
(Lest your offspring never die). She dies later, anyway.
Lobster baby, born from the gardener's wife.

*Jemilea Wisdom-Baako*

# my mother has cold hands

i blame her      mother      for not teaching her
     how to hold      us      or herself
   together.     wonder if     pregnancy
    broke her      promise     to never let anyone
  in.      sometimes      i don't believe
she could feel     me     kick. feel me at all.
   she is always cleaning     moaning     about the mess
we make.      we are      clutter
     spilling out     in front of company.
        i am growing     dust
  from being
       untouched

         yet she hoards me
     as if one day     i will be     useful.
   we are both     still
         waiting.

*Natalie Linh Bolderston*

# Hoa lồng đèn

She could grow them from a small cutting. In England
they had another name, but her daughter called them ballerina flowers.
In her garden in Sóc Trăng, she fed their roots with cold jasmine dregs.
Only she knew about the milk teeth buried and staining
beneath every bush, how each tooth foretold—*a loss in the family*.
Each morning, she left all the doors open—*to let the spirits out*.
In the kitchen, the smell of mint and rain swelled
through fish sauce and five-spice. The night she fled,
she whispered her grandchildren's names into the wet ground,
the only part of them the earth could keep safe.

     In a hospital bed in England, she imagines the bushes
without her: pink petals spiralling, like scraps of her blouse. Teeth
lodged in the throats of street dogs. She lets her coverlet fall.
Years before, the whole garden ignites.

---

Hoa lồng đèn: Vietnamese name for fuchsia.

*Sarala Estruch*

# turtle

is it because he left
so suddenly & irrevocably
that i have lived my life
on land watching
the collapse of water
a body rushes forward
in a curl of saline froth
then retreats—
there is the retreat
knowing this:
each salted step
the careful equilibrium
in me
in you
abandon our shells
we keep as armour
& love

abandoned us
(twice)
as a sea creature
the slow rise &
the way
to embrace another
& desire
always
—
i measure with scales
not to crush
me
& you
(never completely)
hard-boned carapaces
deflecting water
in equal measure

*Leo Boix*

## My Mother on a Diving Board

A leap away from becoming ghost.
She stood erect, her floral bathing suit,
sugared marigolds, a petal cap. She knew
it wouldn't last. *¡Saltá, mamá!*—jump.
Her red blotched arms in precise positions,
her weak body giving way, slowly going
forward. Below her, a mirror reflected

forward. Below her, a mirror reflected
her weak body giving way, slowly going.
Her red blotched arms in precise positions.
It wouldn't last—*¡Saltá, mamá!*—jump.
Sugared marigolds, a petal cap. She knew,
she stood erect, her floral bathing suit,
a leap away from becoming ghost.

*André Naffis-Sahely*

# A Kind of Love

We loved luxury and ate like pigs,
but our room, unborn as yet,
was bare; it was a new building,
and when we moved in, the landlord

looked us over and said: 'no noise
after eleven please'. Obediently,
for the most part, we adhered,
and kept the ancient record player

(among the only things of mine
to survive the neglect and the moths)
at its lowest; although money
was scarce, vinyl records were cheap

and we took advantage.
Halfway through the tenancy,
I got your name mixed up with
another woman's and, quite rightly,

without a word, you took your leave;
taking very little except the needle
you knew full well was irreplaceable,
unlike our short–lived kind of love.

*Leicester*

*Sarala Estruch*

# My Indian grandmother

isn't Indian.

She turns up at my mother's flat

five weeks after my father's death,

majestic with silver curls

like a taller version of the Queen.

*Call me Gran.* I struggle to greet her.

My father never mentioned her

or any family member. My mother

shakes her hand with poise

while, in the kitchen, the kettle screams.

My Indian grandmother takes me

      shopping for the day. *You can choose*

*anything you like*. By the dress rack

      she has a million questions.

She wants to know my favourite everything

      at the Pick 'N' Mix aisle.

I fill the paper bag, at her insistence,

      with pear drops and marshmallow twists,

don't tell her I'm not interested in things

      as I used to be: that liquorice,

for instance, doesn't taste as sweet

      and red and green have lost

their radiance.

In the back of the taxi, her head turned

    absorbing London streets

I get a closer look—regal neck

    and silver locks, pale skin

gently creped. It's strange to think

    my father's hair will never grow white,

that his skin won't soften and fold

    into itself like a rose that holds

onto its stalk long after passing its peak.

*Nadine Aisha Jassat*

# The Time Traveller

*for Geraine*

She returns with a shock:
waking in a reclining chair,
wondering
how she found herself there.

It is my turn to welcome her.
To watch as she searches
for my name in the air,
her mind scrambling, trying to place
the syllables,
      the date,
            my grown-up face.

Once I'm sure she recognises me,
I offer her a cup of tea,
          my smile,
pulled taut as the line of her memory,
beginning to recede,
as she takes in her gathered family

and reminds me to offer our guests.

I know her blend by heart:
Yorkshire, lightly brewed, milky,
and stirred with a sugar
and a half.

Her own, particular, recipe.
This is how she taught me.

Even when she can no longer
remember my name,
she'll know this taste.

Every traveller needs a rest stop,
a space to lay their head.

Today,
she takes her pause with me;
her face smiling as she sips
        milk and sugar,
                warmth and tea.

Draws it through her lips
like breath.

Sighs, turns to me
and says:

        'That's love, that is.
        That's love right there.'

*Charlotte Baldwin*

# Have You Seen the Mushroom Man?

The night my blind grandmother
died, I saw him. I walked to the copse,
slipper-clad, to cry without waking
the house, and there he was—
rising out of the soil,
unhooking himself from his ring of white,
domed troops, clambering
boneless and ghost-fleshed
to comb his long fingers
through the trees' loose hair.

He raised a spindly-finger
to my salt-tracked cheeks
and exhaled, his breath smelled
as she did those last days:
of must and ferment, threaded
with a tang of something
familiar, the smell of a place
unfolding in the air like a map—
a place I could never have been to

but felt I knew, a place of moonless
root-streets, lit only by their own whiteness
where the old became new, the place
each maggot longed to return to,
pried every flesh hole to find again.
Staring into his loamy eyes,

I pictured her running on wet feet
through streets so soft it would not matter
that she could not see, she could fall and get up,
over and over, unhurt, while beetles
marched past on parade.
The tight cage of her bones

gradually opened to let her grow
back into the light as something new.

*Raymond Antrobus*

## Maybe I could love a man

I think to myself
sitting with cousin Shaun in the Spanish Hotel

eating red snapper and rice and peas as Shaun says
*you talk about your father a lot* but I wasn't

talking about my father, I was talking about the host
on 'Smile Jamaica' who said to me on live TV

*If you've never lived in Jamaica you're not Jamaican,*
I said, *my father born here, he brought me back every year*

*wanting to keep something of his home in me*
and the host sneered. I imagine my father laughing

at all the TVs in heaven. He knew this kind of question,
being gone ten years, people said *you from foreign now.*

Cousin Shaun lifts his glass of rum, says *why does anyone*
*try to change their fathers.* Later, it is enough

for me to sit with Uncle Barry as he tells me in his bravado
about the windows he bricked, thrown out of pubs

for standing ground against National Front. His name
for my father was 'Bruck' *because man always ready*

*to bruck up tings* but I know my Uncle is just trying
to say *I miss him.* Look what toughness does

to the men we love. Me and Cousin Shaun are both trying to hold them.
But if our fathers could see us, sitting

in this hotel, they would laugh, not knowing
what else to do. But I'll walk away knowing

there are people here that remember my father,
people who know who I am, who say

our grandfathers used to sit on that hill
and slaughter goats, while our fathers held

babies and their drinks, waving goodbye
to the people on Birch hill who are and are not us.

*Joe Carrick-Varty*

## All of a Sudden

I run my thumb along the jagged edge of the key
I will remove from the bunch any second now.

We've left Hammersmith, six stops to go,
when a text comes through from my father:

an apology for not meeting me
at the Duke for the United game three years ago tonight,

and all of a sudden—because things happen
all of a sudden: like my father breathing

then not breathing, like my father deciding
he might want to die then deciding he definitely wants to die,

and everything in between—all of a sudden
the empty flat I'm whizzing towards,

its cupboards and kettle and bread bin and cat
and smells draped over half-open bedroom doors,

begins to resemble the tiniest of deaths.
Buckle up, kiddo,

there's light at the end of this swinging carriage
if you'll only crane your neck to see.

*Dai George*

# Reclaiming the View

At her graveside I'm without walls. Safe
from the churn of claim and counterclaim,
I hand myself over to what there is:

six trim mountains overlapping,
the town below, its vest of rain.
I sit on her marble roof and hold

a census of the trees. Here flowerless,
there Nordic in their bristling green;
to her left a spritz of elderflower-white

bubbling off the boughs. Her grave
restores the land to decency. She lived
the life for which I'd fight, but knew

no other way. Eventually the rain
will send me spoiling down the valley
into the fractious theatre of claims

but on her grave top I'm unmanned.
Here there is just the fact of her
bones cuddling under me;

spring lambs the hill over
and, around me, headstones:
their small, laconic messages.

# THREE

*"All numbers are divisible by one"*

# Some Friends

Friend who is dead. Friend who stopped taking antidepressants. Friend who celebrates you at every opportunity. Friend who binge-drinks on Fridays and Saturdays. Facebook friend who is not a friend. Friend who is more like family, which is to say you hardly speak. Friend who is no longer a friend after the invoicing incident. Friend who is no longer a friend because you didn't visit her in hospital. Friend who is no longer a friend because she changed the terms and conditions of friendship, and you chose not to renew your subscription. Friend you make art and money with. Friend who is also your lover. Friend who was once your lover. Friend who is more than a friend, but not your lover. Friend who is also black and gay and a poet. Straight friend who shares your bed. Friend getting married. Other friend getting married. Married friend who had her baby early. Pregnant, unmarried friend, moving from her mother's to her man's house. Friend you met at the Houses of Parliament and asked to go for a drink because you fancied him, who has become such a dear friend, and you think sometimes it's okay to think with your dick. Friend who is a mentor. Friend you admire. Friend you might be to yourself.

*Ian Humphreys*

# Bare branch

I once knew a woman with fine elbows.
     She was visiting her dead grandparents.
On tip-toe she swayed in the bamboo grove, watchful,
     as I tiled the roof of my new house.
Uncle read my face—foretold marriage
     and a son with builder's hands.

This woman did not smoke; I liked that.
     She made me bitter melon soup, old style.
I studied her methods of washing rice, dicing
     pork; her strong, clean hair.
She was not too fat, not too thin.
     She wore purple running shoes: Adidas.

One morning, the woman pointed to the road.
     *It floods in winter and the village rests*
*alone for months*, she said. *What would we do then?*
     *Repair uncle's pigsty*, I replied. *Chop kindling.*
*Perhaps mah-jong*
     *if we can find a fourth player.*

Like others before her, she was no gambler.
　　　　She boarded the weekend bus
to Shanghai, found a job dusting iPhones. In spring,
　　　　she returned with a husband who worked
on an assembly line—making buttons
　　　　　　　　for Samsung tablets and iPads.

*That man has the hands of a woman*, Uncle laughed
　　　　into his cracked shaving mirror.
*How can he build her a home?* I invited them both
　　　　to play mah-jong but suffered
a tension headache. Each shuffle of the tiles clattering
　　　　　　　　like tiny feet through the house.

---

In China, a *bare branch* is a man who neither marries nor fathers children
and so does not add fruit to the family tree.

*Stephen Sexton*

# Segue

For the boys with the frog this is it.
No one mostly, older girls sometimes
pass on the straggle of back lanes
and it's for the birds what they talk about.
This variety of August
is untroubled surfaces, fields
of barley at the elbow
and within a stroll, a starve
of waste ground fly-tippers rust
their ancient engines on.
A boulder of liver-spotted granite,
a thumbprint on the belly of a frog.
The boys who carry ruin in their pockets
are becoming other people.

Samphire in the copper pan,
a splendour of salmon.
He's in traffic on the bridge
and this is years from then,
but cruelty is a time traveller.
It is paper, cotton, leather, doves,
the slope of Monte Carlo,
chanterelles, the Shangri-Las,
the valley of the Rhône,
the Wichita Lineman
and its baritone guitar.
A knock at the door, she goes,
and a one and a two and a
one two three four.

*Nick Makoha*

# Pythagoras' Theorem

$$a^2 + b^2 = c^2$$

$a^2$

Remember that summer when
edges went? The whole night
became concentrated darkness,
a neon moon against a pitch sky
(not enough to light the backboard).
Bills not paid but we were up by
two in the third game of the best of seven.

$b^2$

Their point guard calling an illegal pick
as we double teamed, breathing like dogs
on a leash. I was staying in the spare room
of your house. Living below the line
like denominators until I learnt Algebra:
from the word *al-jabr*—the reunion
of broken parts. Your nephew, the third man,
floated by (a silver shadow) and drained
a three crunch through the chains.

$c^2$

His motto, *Those who lack the courage*
*will always find a philosophy to justify it.*
It is a state of being unrestricted.
My wife's fortnightly child-support cheques
last three weeks. All numbers are divisible
by one: the act of being divided. Isn't the God
of the Hebrews also the God of Islam?
We are at right angles the sum of each other.
And then there is zero (that empty place),
where heat and light are meaningless.

*Raymond Antrobus*

# For Rashan Charles

And after the black boy is
strangled by police, after

the protests, where a man
with his Rottweiler on an iron leash

yells, "let's go mash up dis city,"
and another crowd bulks,

the parents of the murdered
beg us not to become

the monsters some think
we already are—even when

the barista shakes her head
at the banners, says, "actually,

police be killing whites too."
Look how scary it is

to be here and know
if we die someone

will make a sound
like her before earth

is tipped over us.
Who hasn't had enough?

Enough burning
bins, enough pushing

shopping trolleys
into static and sirens?

Who isn't chanting:
*enough, enough,*

*enough.* Throwing spells.
The rebellious

holding what they can
in front of a supermarket

or police station
or voting booth. I am

kind to the man
sitting next to me

in C.L.R. James Library, even if
his breathing disturbs me.

Can we disagree graciously.
I am tired of people

not knowing the volume
of their power. Who doesn't

deserve
some silence at night?

Rachel Bower

# Riches

> *when I waked*
> *I cried to dream again*
> — William Shakespeare, *The Tempest*

We spend sweet days by the river, dangling toes,
licking ice-cream, peek-a-boo in the shade.

Sleep brings night sweats and days of others,
angry bellies shouting for food. A toolbox is flung
and cracks the head of my pregnant sister

I'm stuck in mud to the knee, grit in my mouth, screaming
without noise, tongue swelling to tyre proportions.

I cry to wake. A hair-clip sticks in the back of my head,
I am chased by boys with guns
sludge sucking to the thigh. I am awake

but running without moving
blood in the mud that slurps to my chest.

Dawn spills on the bed and wakes me,
her small body curled into mine.

*Meena Kandasamy*

# The Wars Come Home

These days I do not read the news.
I stay at home, all day, every day
and dream of monsoons back home
as London rains on my window.

I watch my baby grow
one day to the next, and think,
this is the closest I will ever get
to bliss, to love, to elusive peace.

I give him a different name
for every play, every bounce,
every little belly laugh, every single
time he smiles, turns his head away.

His father marvels at the many names
I make up on the spot.

Then, one evening, we are looking at him,
tenderness gushing, time standing still—
a baby sleeping on his tummy, his head
buried between his arms, his squidgy
legs in navy shorts—and we look
to each other, say what we both
think. What breaks our hearts, what
makes us move closer to each other.
For this, we do not make up names.

Our baby, sleeping, an enactment
of that little boy washed ashore.
Our baby, sleeping, making us mourn.
Our baby, sleeping, and at that moment
we only see Aylan, Aylan Kurdi, we weep
at a world that has failed them all.

*Anthony Anaxagorou*

# From Here the Camera Crew

look like good news
from the room above
father yells
we're lucky to live in a democracy
          and I believe
the last July of an octogenarian
mourning what could never be
a sparrow delaying its lift
as if apologising to the oak tree
for having to die in the exact place
it was born.

They're sipping Old Fashioned
in their gardens tonight
deckchairs facing the sun
father yells
we're lucky to live in a democracy
          and I believe
the body of a boy in Dalston
the brightness of a screen
a police officer's hands black
as a belt        it's true
worms have learnt to dig
themselves out of the sweetest fruits.

...

Across the flyover a tower
crammed what hurt it knew
into a flame          politicians pick
soundbites from out their crooked teeth
squinting at the brightness of a screen
our nation a slow animal
unable to digest anymore meat.

*Dai George*

# The Park in the Afternoon

By the goats, a high-vis warden
tweezers litter with glacial care.
Men bear tins of Scrumpy Jack aloft
to salute Ol' Blue Eyes as he spreads
the news from a battered tape machine.
Their conductor lies in the regal grass
crafting languorous signals from a spliff.

On the lunchtime news, a minister
reviled my productivity:
*sleepwalking into a crisis*
is how he described the nation's plight
when output fails to tack with growth.
Watching a duckling wobble afloat
as sun glints, useless, on the pond,

I see his point. Diverse and splendid
things have brought us here, we heathens
in the Christendom to come. The drunk,
the retired, the roistering lads
bunking off early with blazer sleeves
riding up their arms—each of us
truant, and gentle for an hour,

our output no more than
what we can make
of the angle of
hurried daylight before
a shower.

*Cristina Navazo-Eguía Newton*

# Hospice

A respite to late summer boredom
was to dare into its fire-gutted wards,
the slow-drip deaths it once tended.

We crossed the threshold in awe,
soft-treading the burnt, broken tiles,
then our reverence waned to the thrill

of trespass and the menace that hung
in the roofless sick rooms. Each wall
was sanctified by its own ruin, random

ghost-patches of colour, and the wild
advance of nature reclaiming
its matter. The game turned against us,

opening silences that could not be shut,
calling names we could not hear
in the noise of our own living. The ashen

dust we kicked up with the dash
and duck of hide and seek made us hack
the coughs of terminal consumptives.

*Sara Hirsch*

# Final Cut

Interior. Morning. Open on human woman standing in front of a full-length mirror. She is dressed for work. You are picturing a pencil skirt. Try harder. Close up on a black leather shoe, shining proudly, catching the light. Close up on an eyebrow, raised, questioning. Close up on a reflection—slowly opening shoulders, straightening back, uncurling the crouch that has been ironed in. Zoom in on clipped fingernails, as they smooth over pinstriped blazer. Pan down tailored trousers and cut to pale blue of tie, dangling between shirted breasts. Cut to briefcase. Cut to cufflinks. Cut to quiff. Narrator tells us that human woman *is working too hard but someone's got to do it*. Narrator speaks in the first person. Narrator is arbitrarily British. Narrator has the confidence of a man in middle management. Narrator could be your mother or your sister or your own internal monologue. Narrator is amazed she got cast. Narrator got her big break and isn't going to waste it. Narrator knows how lucky she is. Narrator is representing her whole gender. Narrator is passing the Bechdel test. Zoom to full body shot. Human man appears in reflection. Narrator sighs. *Too good to be true.* Slowly, deliberately, human woman strips off suit until lace is revealed. Red. To match the cheeks. Suit is handed over. Cufflinks unclipped and quiff smoothed to flattened fringe. Human woman watches human man get dressed for the day. He is wearing it wrong. Zoom past her naked torso to catch the knot of his tie. The cut of his smile. The raise of an eyebrow. Abruptly, to rousing music, our hero leaves for work. Credits role. Names of men scroll as human woman scrambles for a dressing gown. Names of male directors, producers, actors, fill the screen. Names of men who provided the costumes. Men who dressed the set, who built the set, who lit the set. Continuity men. Sound men. Special effects men and stunt men—who were there in case human woman needed to do anything dangerous. Men who provided the catering. Who wrote the script. Who scouted locations. Names of men who didn't even make the movie, just men who ought to be noted. Local men. Famous men. Men who worked in the movie theatre, who sold the tickets, who operated the projector. Men who went to watch the movie. Men who identified with the main character. Who saw themselves in the story, who liked the ending, who would recommend this one to their friends. So many names flood the screen you can barely see human woman dancing awkwardly in the background in underwear she didn't choose. Somewhere, in a boardroom, this movie is approved and applauded. It is rated M for Men and it is an instant, multi-award-winning blockbuster hit. It is decided that this movie is so good and so relatable it will be shown all day, everyday, in every movie theatre, airplane, office, living room and laptop in the world. Cut to human woman, hand pressed against the inside of the screen, sweating on the glass, breathing heavily, nearly naked. The names continue to flow. Lower the camera's gaze, guiltily. Narrator is silent. Fade to black.

*Nina Mingya Powles*

# Mixed Girl's Hakka Phrasebook

*after Sennah Yee*

Words I know in Hakka:

One, Two, Three, Four, Five, Sit down, It tastes good, Please, Thank you.

Words I do not know in Hakka:

How are you, It's so good to see you, How did you sleep, It is such a beautiful morning, Did you hear the rain, Did you have dreams, What would you like to eat, I'm sorry, Can you speak a little slower, Can you say that again, Can you write that down, What does that mean, I can't speak, I'm sorry, I wish I could speak, How do you say, What do you know, Have you ever, Have you ever been, Have you ever seen, Have you ever felt, How long ago, When was the first time, What was it like, Do you still, Do you remember who, Do you remember the way, Do you remember when you were a child, Do you remember your home, Do you remember leaving, Do you remember the colour, Do you remember the sound of, Do you remember the taste of, Do you remember the smell of, Do you remember the name, Do you remember.

Stephen Sexton

# A Pledge

I say, let's not fell a sequoia
or any other huge and ancient tree
and chisel out a bungalow to live in.
Sweetheart, amigo, it would take forever.

We're not lumberjacks or surgeons
or carpenter ants or blizzards or today, anyway,
death galloping through the woods
in the black dress of a wildfire.

Yes, each dead bird is one
in the allness of birds
but such a tree is a mortgage
of sawdust and sap,

and suppose he's elderly:
the man dying in his parlour
in the body a skeleton
floats to the surface of?

If the sound of chopping wood
is on the air, holy men say
the soul cannot escape,
and agony, agony, but even

the unsuperstitious are suffering
on Tuesdays or Thursdays
acutely in bedrooms
near scarecrows or not near them.

Is it moral to abstract oneself
from someone else's suffering
or the opposite? The answer
bolts like Fido from his master

and will not heel. And besides,
it's passé: living in the woods
with its dreamboat night sky
and its fragrant respiration

and and and and and and and
you might say, excuses.
And were it not for the cherish
of your hi-vis and hardhat,

the promise of your axe in the air,
I'd have said, let's not, and meant it
and swung no such almighty cut
into our luxury mausoleum.

*Rachael Allen*

# Untitled

Ants congregate around her arm.
A figure I admire silently, cast in stone,
abundantly, but without luxury.
He swims and the lights come on,
how the moon indicates one trail
through the path of delicate insects.
The woods walk at a slant, a hill of
trees that are drunk, unstable blocks of green.
What remains stable in the water,
a figure with her arms around her face,
a figure with her arms outstretched.

# FOUR

*"It starts at the rumor of another epoch"*

*Caroline Hardaker*

# On Opening a Love Note Delivered by Snail

I might just be a simple mushroom, bruised by weathers
and tipped by gloom, but you're one too (though far more moon-like).
I've heard you pulse your hyphae-strings many times,
tripping out a melody for my 'shroomy ears to hear.
I sang back every night to your fruiting body, gills rippling.
You've been eyeing me too, lifting up your pearl skirt
a little further each day, you flirt.

You don't belong in that distant dirt. Look over this deciduous lap
and see—I'm dipping my cap to you. It's taken me two weeks
to twist my stem down and around—
I'm sponge, and open to any crushing boot to stamp your way.
I'd choose to be the one to break in two,
if it gave you an extra day.

And listen, if we both move, migrate, we can start our patch
in half the time! Picture the young spores we'll have—
little meteorites, throbbing mycelium love notes like stars
to illuminate our wilting days. They might inherit your egg-shine,
or the convex of my cap. They'll bulb up, all clean, and we'll rub
up the cusps of each other until we stick, blunting memory-smudges
of where we've been, the underneaths only we've seen, all raw ribs.

...

I can't wait to metabolise matter with you, consume a legume or two.
We can be casual at first, bloom, and then shrink under tented matters
as we feed our buttoned galley, the family.
I get softer with age, so be tender with me. I take in the sun
through a skinless skull—so consider this sensitivity when you respond.
For us the earth is quick, and we won't be standing here long.
Send the messenger snail back forthwith, with your answer—

he's not the quickest, you know,
and for us time is of the essence.

*Khairani Barokka*

# Hello, Sequelae

Because another storm is humming,
you squat by a creek, chin out.
Tease the fringes of river intoxicants,
thumb and forefinger dunked in the wet,
breathing air that makes you a statistic.
Low to the ground, lung-filling spatter.

Pry yourself from rushing water,
face what the minnow knows,
what stoic ducks understand,
what treebanks feel as a seeping-in.

A falling outwards of equilibrium
hunts a sore chest, senses insects
leaving the grounds where you make
fast homestead, temporary, walls
already too pale, too fading, ivory
as the full teeth of ghosts.

Find heat-emanating bodies,
find axe and blanket.
No hurtling yourself under tables,
you have always been so open
to skin-piercing things, there is no
safe house. In your hands
is how to seed earth.
You have always known how
to tell time by sky.

*Carrie Etter*

# Parable

The water in the boat's hold is five feet high, and I have a thimble for the bailing. Each day the duty roster remains the same: I take the burden longer than any member of my crew. Weeks pass with no appreciable progress, and at least daily the tiny steel cup slips from my fingers, to be rescued from the murk after lost minutes, sometimes an hour. After months, we find a shipwreck survivor on a dinghy, and in gratitude he offers me his bucket. I throw it into the sea to show him the magnitude of my work.

*Charlotte Baldwin*

# With my lips pressed to the ear of the Earth

I kneel down and confess.

### APOLOGY

'I am sorry, mother, but…'

1.  I will use old trees to write this down
2.  The roads offered speed with a side of fumes, and I said *yes*
3.  Everything I ate came wrapped—like an offering—in plastic

There is no reply.

### APPEASEMENT

I tell her that since I gave up office life, the rooms in my heart have ivy
reaching around the windows, and I know this was a gift from her,
and I am here, under the beech tree, to give thanks.

I tell her of the morning I stood here watching a deer
surge over a barbed wire fence in the snow—
how I forgot to move my feet.

### LOVE

I say it aloud, *I love you.*
The soft soil below me
gives a little, cradles the cap
of each mushroom knee.

It's not enough. What I want to say
runs for a path through the long grass,
finds itself so wide it cannot pass
through the field-gate of my mouth.

REMORSE

I speak with my hands. Breaking
the pastry crust of the topsoil,
peeling out rusted ringpulls,
packing black crescents behind
each white nail. I am hugging
what cannot be hugged, and it is sweeter
than the taste of nectar from the trumpet
of a nettle flower, and I am sorrier
than any child who ever learned too
late what it means to be ungrateful.

*Rowan Evans*

# Habitual Statements

It isn't late, I am remote, in the skill
    of sun-shadow.

◇

The St Kilda wren, gathering in size
    so that one year it might depart.

◇

Certain things were beautiful, not only
    metered, according to sleep.

◇

Such a simple weight, the wren. It starts
    at the rumor of another epoch.

◇

MARINA, MIDAS, blue tower of cirrus.

◇

There was no canto of the underworld
    and the wren replayed its footage.

◇

Without foothold, what is this residence,
     its gauze exacted to flight?


◇


How total to forsake, *visited upon the earth*.
     *In motions and formations*, the poem thinks.


◇


The wren collects, and night is miles away.

*Rachael Allen*

# Untitled

Chaos on the hillside,
green chaos. The forest
is a chamber, the blue of
a dilapidated stream.
Sky flicks through crowns
like a damaged wire.
In the periphery of vision
branches hold utterances.
Steep paths undetermined,
translucent, artificial indigo,
bluish tipped and baked.
Horizon custard, glowing
mute citrine on the horizon.
The lower canopy dampens
crayon green and lucid.
The forest floor simmers,
the serum of a coal fire,
an internalised rusting.

*Harry Josephine Giles*

# Volume

This stane is lood. In hids howe rubbit
intae a grander stane, hid lins lood.
The howe is lood; the grander stane, lood;
an the tide twal feet awa turnin here
on hids twice-a-day band is lood. Lood,
the dear spreid o tangle; lood, the trinkle
o iper fae the field abuin; lood, the runic
track o a chaldro in the lood sand;
lood, the three-quarter sun. Whan thir nae a body
tae hear, aa this an more is lood eneuch
tae daive, tae mak bleed, tae brak bane, tae shak
apairt the tentless hearan objeck, that's no here.

———

This stone is loud. In its hollow rubbed into a bigger stone, it rests loudly.
The hollow is loud; the bigger stone, loud; and the tide twelve feet away
turning here on its twice-a-day hinge is loud. Loud, the expensive spread of
seaweed; loud, the trickle of slurry from the field above; loud, the runic track
of an oystercatcher in the loud sand; loud, the three-quarter sun. When there's
nobody to hear, all this and more is loud enough to deafen, to make bleed, to
break bone, to shake apart the unwary listening object, who's not here.

Nancy Campbell

# Lost

*for Matthew Teller*

Matthew's flown to the Falkland Islands
to record Magellanic penguins braying in York Bay.
Will his BBC boom, fluffy as a fledgling,
confuse the birds? Penguins have encountered
their fair share of odd, man–made objects
since that infamous leather football was
kicked about on the ice-shelf by explorers
before they came home to fight a war.
Just a lark in those days, men versus penguins—
just a game. At primary school I learnt to imitate
their waddle, keeping my flippers stiff, my feet flat.
I ate chocolate biscuits with terrible jokes
on the wrappers: *What do you call five-hundred penguins
in Trafalgar Square? Lost.*
      Now, thanks to *Planet Earth*,
I can live with the colony through a polar winter
in one evening and I see it is no joke:
sitting in shit, and calling in vain for your chick,
shivering in storms and shrinking from predators—
good luck if you are stuck on the outskirts
of the circle. In kinder weather, Matthew's mic
will record the coming and going of cruise passengers—
modern pilgrims, who have circled the globe
to huddle in Bluff Cove for three hours
in adoration of Gentoos. Their guides say,
*Take nothing but photos. Don't leave rubbish behind.*
They'll say it again to those who land the next day
wearing identical expedition jackets.

Their cameras won't capture the landmines
dumped in the dunes on orders from Whitehall—another war,
back when I was discovering how to be a penguin,
how to spot the difference between Emperors
and Kings, how to deliver a punchline.

*Cristina Navazo-Eguía Newton*

# We Drive Past

The surveyor setting up a theodolite
to establish the gradient of souls and soil

a spirit level measuring the spirit level

A manmade line of poplars
poor in its stiff arrangements of missing oriels

preconceived computer rhythms stuck
from another driver's radio

Bluebells thrive and will thrive
again on the death of daffodils

in short sequence between the hunger gaps

The long dark tunnel slow down
in case something is coming

the pendulum pulse of 40-30-40

A clump of trees clogged with
empty nests and cold spring

buzzard, pigeon, helicopter

Fourteen bends before the 303
Thin teeth of reforested land

Lorries attempting to overtake
but lacking the power thereof

Speedcamera bats latched on to street lamps

Dirty whites of early blossom
Gorse dividing the coming from the going

Dead tractor towed from its final stop

Burst carcasses and rags of roadkills
reminders of what we are capable of doing

Juggernaut smouldering on the roadside

Stonehenge stalled queues of returning cars
Pacing tourists fastened to recordings

The dormant antlers of screen-wipers

army vehicle slowdown warnings
of target practice and landmines

You focused on arriving, silence clamped
on what brings the distance in

*Khairani Barokka*

# remaining outpost

snow presents itself on green leaves,
rain seeps into dry season. no time
left for bereavement of species
and language, my father cracks us
open a rainforest plant he's forgotten
the name of, brought home to city.

inside, two translucent alien orbs
large with seed. sweet and off-white
as kelengkeng, longer and more oval.
orange, sappy, with tang, another fruit:
liwat, yet untranslated into english,
unextracted from en masse to shelve
groceries, sliver of its bright saliva
spun out. the hooting relief of these
mysteries entering our consciousness,
while plain as the sun for people freed
from our kind of terrible, jealous
and guzzling, miserly, prickly with sodium
laureth sulfate and parabens, awash
in a drowning, online sales for clothing
a spike of adrenaline, the woods
as a set of conquerable names.

*Jenna Clake*

# Elegy for Balto from the Bottom of a Frozen Lake

and later we all fell down with a sickness and the antitoxin
was six-hundred miles away if you are a wolf-dog then I am
walking along aisles of chocolate bars picking them up and
putting them straight down I believe my body should fit
behind a face cloth and that is why I'd make a terrible parent
if you are a bear fight then I am willing to lose and limp
home without you tell me how a dog's face is prettier than
mine if you are a dusty piano then I am false markers on the
route back if you are light refracted through a broken glass jar
then I am a deep growling an injured paw an uncredited
snow goose racing to beat you and never quite making it

Rachel Bower

# Haibun Meltdown

*Svalbard archipelago, Norway*

Picture the game where you rip a piece of newspaper in half every time
the music stops. The children crowd unnaturally close on tiny pieces of print.
Soon, they will start to fall off. I catch one, collect his tears, but do not know
where to tip them. I decide to freeze them in little blocks for later. The party
is ruined, children flapping everywhere.


*dazzling blue ice-caps*


*cracked to polystyrene bits*


*floating in blackness*

# CONTRIBUTORS

*with warmth & gratitude*

*Rachael Allen* is the poetry editor for *Granta* magazine and books. Her first collection of poems, *Kingdomland*, was published by Faber & Faber.

*Anthony Anaxagorou* is a British-born Cypriot poet, fiction writer, essayist, publisher, and poetry educator. He is the artistic director of Out-Spoken and publisher of Out-Spoken Press.

*Raymond Antrobus* is a British-Jamaican poet from London. He is the author of *To Sweeten Bitter* and *The Perseverance* (winner of The Ted Hughes Award and The Rathbone Folio 2019).

*Dean Atta* was shortlisted for the Polari First Book Prize for his debut poetry collection *I Am Nobody's Nigger*. His debut novel, *The Black Flamingo*, is published by Hodder Children's Books.

*Charlotte Baldwin* is an arts programmer, creative writing tutor & dog-walker. As Gypsy Rose Poetry, she performs everywhere from the National Poetry Library to nursing homes.

*Khairani Barokka* is an Indonesian writer and artist in London and Modern Poetry in Translation's Inaugural Poet-In-Residence. Her works include *Indigenous Species* and debut collection *Rope*.

*Emily Blewitt*'s poetry collection, *This Is Not A Rescue*, was published by Seren Books in 2017. She is the poetry submissions editor for *New Welsh Reader*.

*Leo Boix* is a Latinx poet born in Argentina and based in the UK. He is the recipient of the Keats-Shelley Prize 2019. Boix's debut collection will be out in 2021 with Chatto & Windus.

*Natalie Linh Bolderston* received the silver Creative Future Writers' Award in 2018 and is a Bi'an Award runner-up. Her pamphlet, *The Protection of Ghosts*, is published with V. Press.

*Rachel Bower* lives in Sheffield. She is a Leverhulme Fellow at the University of Leeds and the author of *Moon Milk* (Valley Press) and *Epistolarity and World Literature* (Palgrave Macmillan).

*Nancy Campbell* is currently the UK's Canal Laureate. Her books include *The Library of Ice* (2018) and *Disko Bay* (2015, shortlisted for the Forward Prize for Best First Collection).

*Joe Carrick-Varty* is an Irish/British poet who lives in London. His debut pamphlet *Somewhere Far* (The Poetry Business) won the 2018 New Poets Prize. He is a founding editor of *bath magg*.

An editor of Oxford Poetry, *Mary Jean Chan* is a poet and Lecturer in Creative Writing (Poetry) at Oxford Brookes University. *Flèche* (Faber & Faber, 2019) is her first book.

*Jenna Clake*'s collection, *Fortune Cookie*, received an Eric Gregory Award from the Society of Authors. A pamphlet of her prose poems, *CLAKE / Interview for*, is published by Verve.

*Sarala Estruch* is a writer and poet from London. She is currently working on her debut collection with the support of a grant from Arts Council England.

*Carrie Etter* is Reader in Creative Writing at Bath Spa University. Her fourth, most recent collection is *The Weather in Normal* (UK: Seren; US: Station Hill, 2018).

*Rowan Evans* is a poet, composer, sound artist and editor of Moot Press. A selection of his work appears in *Penguin Modern Poets 7: These Hard and Shining Things* (Penguin, 2018).

*Dai George*'s first collection was *The Claims Office* (Seren, 2013), and his work has been widely published in magazines and anthologies. He works as reviews editor for *Poetry London*.

*Harry Josephine Giles* is a writer and performer from Orkney who lives in Leith; they are the author of *Tonguit* (Freight Books) and *The Games* (Out-Spoken Press).

*Remi Graves* is a London based poet and drummer. A former Barbican Young Poet, her work has been featured on BBC Radio 4, at Tate Modern, St Paul's Cathedral and more.

*Caroline Hardaker*'s poetry has been published worldwide. Her poetry collection (*Bone Ovation*) was published in 2017 by Valley Press, and her second is forthcoming in winter 2019.

*Sara Hirsch*'s poetry has appeared in journals/anthologies in four continents. She has two published collections (Burning Eye Books) and is co-founder of *Motif Poetry*.

*Ian Humphreys*' debut collection, *Zebra*, is published by Nine Arches Press (2019). A fellow of The Complete Works, his poems feature in *Ten: Poets of the New Generation* (Bloodaxe).

*Omotara James* is the author of the chapbook *Daughter Tongue*. The daughter of Nigerian and Trinidadian immigrants, she was selected as a 2019 finalist for the Brunel International African Poetry Prize.

*Nadine Aisha Jassat* is an award-winning writer based in Scotland, and the author of *Let Me Tell You This* (404 Ink), described by Makar Jackie Kay as a "punchy, powerful debut."

*Meena Kandasamy* is a Chennai-born, London-based author who has published two collections of poetry. Her latest novel, *When I Hit You*, was shortlisted for the Women's Prize for Fiction 2018.

*Bryony Littlefair* is a poet, community centre worker and workshop facilitator living in South London. Her pamphlet *Giraffe* won the Mslexia Pamphlet Prize in 2017 and is published with Seren.

*Nick Makoha*'s debut collection, *Kingdom of Gravity*, was shortlisted for the 2017 Felix Dennis Prize for Best First Collection and nominated by *The Guardian* as one of the best books of the year.

*André Naffis-Sahely* is the author of *The Promised Land* (Penguin) and *The Other Side of Nowhere* (Rough Trade Editions). He is the editor of *The Heart of a Stranger: An Anthology of Exile Literature*.

*Cristina Navazo-Eguía Newton* is the author of three poetry collections. *Cry Wolf* (Templar Poetry) received a Straid Award. She is currently a Creative Writing Ph.D. student at Cardiff University.

*Alycia Pirmohamed* is a poet and Ph.D. student living in Scotland. She is the author of the chapbook *Faces that Fled the Wind* (forthcoming, BOAAT Press).

*Nina Mingya Powles* is a poet and writer of mixed Malaysian-Chinese heritage, born in New Zealand, living in London. She is the founding editor of *Bitter Melon* 苦瓜.

*Stephen Sexton*'s first book, *If All the World and Love Were Young* is published by Penguin and is shortlisted for the Forward Prize for Best First Collection.

*Jennifer Lee Tsai* is a Liverpool-based poet, critic, and editor. She is a Complete Works fellow and a Ledbury Poetry Critic. Her debut poetry pamphlet *Kismet* is published by ignitionpress.

*Jemilea Wisdom-Baako* is a British–Jamaican poet. A Callaloo Fellow and The Watering Hole Fellow, she was recently shortlisted for the Rebecca Swift Women's Poet Prize.

*Anthology Editor*

*Michelle Tudor* is an editor from England. She is the co-founder and editor of Platypus Press and the literary journal *wildness*.

# ACKNOWLEDGEMENTS

*with thanks to the following publications*

Grateful acknowledgement is made to the following editors and publications in which the below poems—sometimes in earlier versions—first appeared. Unless noted otherwise, copyright for the poems is held by the individual poets.

*Journals*

'Riches' by Rachel Bower, in *Popshot Magazine* (Issue 21, Autumn 2018)

'Volume' by Harry Josephine Giles, in *Irish Pages* (Vol. 10, No. 2)

'Bare branch' by Ian Humphreys, in *The Poetry Review* (Vol. 107, No. 4)

Omotara James, 'Exhibition of the Queered Woman' in *American Chordata* (Issue Six, Winter 2018)

Meena Kandasamy, 'The Wars Come Home' in *International Gallerie* (Vol. 20, No. 2)

Nick Makoha, 'Pythagoras Theorem' in *adda* (March 2017)

Alycia Pirmohamed, 'Fire Starter' from *Prairie Schooner* (Vol. 92, No. 1)

Stephen Sexton, 'Segue' in *Poetry Ireland Review* (Issue 123)

Jennifer Lee Tsai, 'The Meaning of Names' in *Oxford Poetry* (XVII.II / Winter 2017–18)

*Books*

'From Here the Camera Crew' reproduced from *After the Formalities* by Anthony Anaxagorou, published by Penned in the Margins. With permission from Penned in the Margins. Copyright © Anthony Anaxagorou, 2019

Platypus Press is an independent publisher of poetry, fiction, and narrative non-fiction established in 2015 and based in Shropshire, England.

platypuspress.co.uk